THE CHANGING F

Oxford Covered Market

Marilyn Yurdan

Series number 63

Robert Boyd
PUBLICATIONS

OTHER TITLES IN THE *CHANGING FACES* SERIES

Published by
Robert Boyd Publications
260 Colwell Drive
Witney, Oxon OX28 5LW

First published 2008
Copyright © Marilyn Yurdan
and *Robert Boyd Publications*

ISBN: 978 1 899536 89 4

Printed and bound in
Great Britain at the
Alden Press, Witney
OX29 0YG

Contents

Cover illustrations

Front cover: Michael Feller with a display of
poultry, November 1998.

Back cover: Bonners Fruiterers in July 1997.

Introduction

Oxford Covered Market was officially opened on 1st November 1774 and is one of the oldest in the country. It was part of the 1771 Mileways Act, an initiative aimed at cleaning up Oxford by removing traders' stalls from the streets and updating the city centre.

As can be seen by looking at street directories, over the years, Market traders have changed considerably. In the early years the goods on sale were almost exclusively foodstuffs or related items such as cooking utensils, kitchenware and baskets. By far the most common were the butchers of all kinds – including purveyors of pork, game, bacon, game. There were also fishmongers, cheese factors and sellers of dairy produce.

Another of the Market's early functions was to serve as a meeting place, where, as in any other market place, announcements could be made and wrong-doers punished.

Gradually, greengrocers, seeds-men, nursery-men and florists moved into the Market along with clothing and footwear outlets, then toy shops, sweetshops, newsagents and tobacconists.

Places to eat began to open up, starting with those catering for the traders themselves and then proper dining rooms. Today the range of places to eat, both sit-in and takeaway, is very wide with traditional dining-room meals, continental style cafés and trendy takeaways.

By the end of the twentieth century the Market consisted of a range of businesses, with the butchers, fishmongers, florists and fruiters now very much in the minority. The current emphasis is on fine food, including continental chocolates, speciality cheeses and designer cakes, and unusual goods like jewellery, high quality leather goods, designer shoes, fun children's clothing and toys.

So much remains to be written about the history of the Market and its traders, the families, change and continuity and the business links forged. What has appeared to date has consisted of articles in scholarly journals. This book contains a record of its every-day life from its opening until the present day.

Virtually every guide book and Internet article on the city centre includes the Market which has become a tourist attraction in its own right with its most of shops and cafés having their own websites and attracting reviews and recommendations.

Although the Covered Market has been described as the Jewel in Oxford's crown, it has a history of conflict, sometimes reacting against the jurisdiction of the University as vested in the Clerks of the Market, but much more frequently in its dealings with the City Council regarding rent increases. It is to be hoped that Oxford Covered Market will weather the storms and continue to attract residents and visitors alike.

Acknowledgements

Thanks are due to Stephanie Jenkins, Chris McDowell and *Newsquest Oxfordshire.*

Further Reading

Town and Gown, eight hundred years of Oxford life, an exhibition at the Bodleian Library, 1982.
Malcolm Graham, "The Building of Oxford Covered Market, 1773-1774", *Oxoniensia* (1970, vol. xxxv: 59-70); and 1979, vol. xliv: 89-91.
Hunt and Co. Directory, various years; *Jackson's Oxford Journal,* various years; *Kelly's Directory,* various years; *Oxford Chronicle* various years; *Oxford Street Directory,* various years; *Robson's Directory,* 1858; *Valter's Post Office Directory,* various years; *Victoria County History of Oxfordshire,* vol iv.

   www.oxford-covered-market.co.uk
   www.oxfordcity.co.uk/shops/market
   www.headington.org.uk/oxon/high/tour/north/market.htm

The Market over the Years

Before the Covered Market, which connects High Street and Market Street, existed the town's market area had spread out along the streets leading from Carfax including Queen Street and St Aldates which were formerly called Butcher Row and Fish Street respectively. According to the terms of a charter of 1355, granted to the University by Edward III, the Chancellor was allowed to regulate market prices to prevent unfair dealing. In this way the Chancellor (or Vice-Chancellor) had powers exercised by magistrates elsewhere. By 1380 there were 16 butchers, 18 fishmongers and 7 grocers in the market areas which spread out around the centre. Two Clerks of the Market (the title was first used in 1513) who had to be a Head of House, MAs or Bachelors of Divinity, Medicine or Law, were appointed to ensure that all trading was done correctly. The Covered Market was constructed in an attempt to clear `untidy, messy and unsavoury stalls` from the main streets as they blocked the traffic. John Gwynn, the architect of Magdalen Bridge, drew up the plans and designed the High Street frontage with its four entrances. In 1772 the newly-formed Market Committee (six of whose members came from the town and six from the University) accepted an estimate of £916.10/- (nine hundred and sixteen pounds ten shillings), for building twenty butchers' shops. Twenty more soon followed and after 1773 meat was only allowed to be sold inside the market. Notices of fines for persons selling fruit, foodstuffs etc outside the Market appeared in *Jackson's Oxford Journal*. Offenders were liable to prosecution and a £5 penalty for each offence, half of which to go to the informant and half to the poor. This edict was challenged from time to time until the late 19th century by those wishing to open shops elsewhere and by their prospective customers who lived in the suburbs at an inconvenient distance from the Covered Market. From this nucleus the Market grew, with stalls for garden produce, pig meat, dairy products and fish. Profits from trading were to be divided evenly between the University and the City. At the start and finishing of trading each day a bell was rung in a turret at the north end. The first Beadle of the Market was William Tubb whose responsibilities included cleansing and rent collection. He lived on the premises and received ten shillings a week from which he had to supply cleaning and maintenance materials.

Apart from clearing up the streets, the Market offered traders and shoppers alike shelter from the weather. Although the estimated cost had been £5,647.15/-, this was reduced to £3,997 when land on the High Street frontage was sold. Among the first shops were forty butchers' shops; these were followed by fishmongers, mercers and grocers. The first stalls, made of timber with lath and plaster cladding, stood on a flagstone floor and had slate roofs. In addition to the stalls there was an open area where traders could sell their wares from baskets or trays. This arena hosted events such as the Quarter Sessions' punishment for two former Militia-men who were 'tried for penalty under Queen Elizabeth' to stand publicly in the pillory in the Market Place for two hours, plus a £10 fine on 17th July 1783, and a man who had stolen a shirt was publicly whipped there in July 1785.

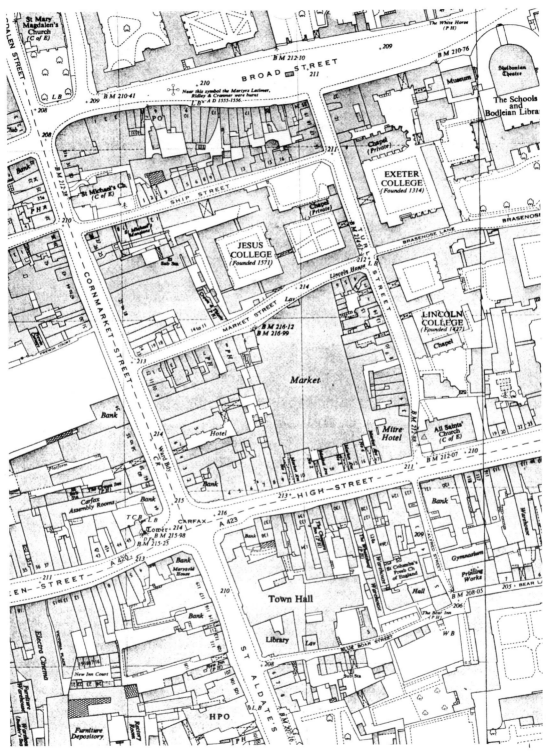

Map to show the position of the Market in the city centre.

An entry in Jackson's Oxford Journal in 1789 records how:

> About noon on Wednesday last, a vulgar mode of Divorce lately adopted, was put into practice here in our New Market Place, before a Multitude of Witnesses. Richard Hawkins, a Canal Navigator-Man, made a public Sale of his wife to William Gibbs, a Mason employed at the works of the Castle.
>
> After a conversation about the payment of 5/- as the purchase money, the old Husband pulled out a Penny Slip and tied around the Waist of his Wife, the end of which he held fast till he had pocketed three shillings in Part, the Purchaser not abounding in Cash. He then put the Cord into the hands of the New Husband and took French leave. The woman immediately called for her second Wedding Ring, which being put on, she eagerly kissed the Fellow with which she walked off, leaving the Spectators in Amazement at such uncommon Assurance.

The *Universal Business Directory* of 1794 has a description of the Market as it then was:

> The old shambles in Butcher Row (Queen Street) are likewise taken away, and a new general market, upon an extensive scale, is erected between the High-street and Jesus College Lane; which market is universally allowed to exceed every thing of the kind in this kingdom. At the south entrance from the High-street it contains forty commodious shops for butchers. North of these are eight others equally commodious; occupied by gardeners, &c. between which are two spacious colonnades for poultry, eggs, bacon, cheese, &c. &c. divided into forty stalls; and beyond these, extending quite to Jesus College Lane, is a large area for country gardeners, fruit, and divers other commodities. There are likewise three avenues running through in direct lines, intersected by another in the middle, affording a free currency of air; and in the front, four elegant and commodious houses have been erected, which give an additional ornament to one of the finest streets in Europe. The open part of this market, fronting Jesus College, is inclosed by an iron palisade; and the avenues opening upon the New Parade in the High-street are secured by iron gates. The whole extent of the ground appropriated to the purpose of erecting this market, is from north to south three hundred and forty-seven feet, and from east to west one hundred and twelve.

In 1808 forty-eight further stalls were added for gardeners and sellers of garden produce and eight years later improved premises for sellers of dairy produce. An extension was built in 1838 with a newer entrance, the present Avenue 1, leading to it. A roof had been added in 1831 and the Avenues were laid out systematically in the course of the 19th century although businesses still operated from stalls rather than shops.

Further extensions and modifications were noted in the local press: the covering of the adjoining Fish Market by a glass roof in 1874; an extension of North-west Avenue of the New Market through to High Street added 19 shops and improved many others in 1881. This new Avenue started at the High Street and ran through the Market between what was Turrill's poultry shop and Lambourn's basket warehouse. A branch avenue was built at the south end. This rebuilding largely did away with the original buildings. In 1881 a new block and south end was added and the following year the last of the 4 principal avenues was added.

In 1884 the *Oxford Chronicle* of 12th January reports how Cross Avenue No 1 (with a high roof like Avenues 1 and 2) was being built and that Cross Avenue No 2 was shortly to be rebuilt. Three years later new Avenues leading into Market Street and a large cross avenue with one smaller one were erected and parts which had been damaged by fire were restored.

In 1889 the City Council took over responsibility from the University which had overseen trading since the Middle Ages, although the position of Clerks of the Market survives to this day. Their only function nowadays is to find out the price of corn twice a year and to announce it at an annual dinner for the colleges' estates bursars as some of the colleges' rents are based on these prices.

In October 1894, *Jackson's Oxford Journal* notes that each shop had now been fitted with patent revolving wood shutters by Hodgkinson of Birmingham.

This postcard of the High Street frontage shows the inconspicuous entrance to the present Avenue 4. In the picture the Mitre Hotel extends westwards above the Market.

Even today a passer-by who is unaware of the location of the Market could easily miss seeing it. Despite considerable Internet coverage and the shops' individual websites, the entrances are still the same, narrow with no external signs or advertisements apart from the Avenue numbers above them to show that it is there. The fact that the Market has continued to prosper even with so little publicity proves its attraction to the shoppers of Oxford and beyond.

Horse-drawn vans delivering to the High Street entraces in 1906.

General view in 1963 when more rent increases (in some cases double), were introduced. The assessment of the new rents at 21/6d a square foot of floor space was intended to bring the rents of all 45 tenants into line.

Women shoppers congregating around the Market Street entrance in 1964.

Market Street entrances in May 1968, showing the new access road on the far right.

In June 1972 the cross-roads of the Market once again acted as a display area when a National Savings stall was set up there. Viscountess Parker and Mr Eric Preece-James, District Commissioner, are shown chatting to Mrs Florence Witteridge of Kenilworth Avenue.

In January 1973, following a letter to the local press, a seat was installed in the centre of the Market.

By May 1982 cracks had begun to show in the 200-year-old outside wall in Market Street near Avenue 2. Timber supports were put in place to keep shoppers safe.

More ancient fabric in another wall of the Market, at the High Street end, in April 1993.

Dr Malcolm Graham, Local Studies Librarian for Oxfordshire, who has done a considerable amount of research into the history of the Market, pictured for an article in the *Oxford Times* in May 1979.

Mary Ann Porter and Tracy Maconochie, two girls who were trapped in the Market after closing time in October 1977 were given a slug of whisky and soda to keep out the cold by Charles Henderson, relief landlord of the Roebuck next door.

One weekend in September 1980 rings and watches worth £8500 were stolen during a night-time raid on Gowing's Jewellers. The thieves smashed three holes in the roof of the Market and used a hook to fish the valuables out of the window display. Nearly 60 Seiko quartz watches were taken and about 50 rings. Mr Gowing said that, although the gates to the Market were locked at night, 'a geriatric could climb in.' No keys to the site were held by either the Police or the Fire Brigade and currently there was one break-in every two weeks. He suggested that the gates be left open in order that the police could patrol the Avenues but some tenants disagreed with this idea, saying that their premises were less secure.

In 1989, after nearly 18 months' negotiations, an agreement with the City Council permitted a 167% rent rise spread over 5 years. Frank Watson, left is shown with Bill Fagg, chairman of the Covered Market sub-committee. Rents have been a problem virtually since the Market opened and continue to be so.

The same year Tom Ellis, manager of the Oxford Craft Centre, predicted that many market traders might be forced to raise their prices, offer poorer service or even in the case of smaller businesses close altogether. He was proved right and his own shop eventually became one of the casualties.

Market tenants celebrating a victory over the Council regarding rates in April 2001. From the left: Colin Bonner (Bonner's greengrocers), Sandie Griffiths (Jemini), Mark Stoker (Hedges Butchers), Alan Lester (Delcoy's) and Mitzi Feller (Feller's Butchers).

By June 2008 the people of Oxford had begun to question seriously whether the Covered Market would continue to exist in its present form. Posters reading 'Save the Covered Market' appeared in the windows of many traders in response to the claim that several shops were in danger of going out of business.

A petition bearing more than 3,500 names was presented to Oxford City Council on behalf of angry shoppers, anxious to defend the Market traders in the face of yet more crippling rent rises. The Jemini flower shop, for example, has been presented with an increase of more than 100 per cent, from £25,000 to £57,000. The petition's signatories said that they 'humbly request the city council will seek to support the Covered Market for the benefit of the community, as an irreplaceable part of Oxford's heritage, by pledging to give a fair deal to traders to protect and enhance the quality and variety of local businesses present in the building today.'

The petition was organized by Conservative Party members and welcomed by the businesses under threat. Fifty-four of the traders appealed against the rises, the Traders' Association took up their complaints and the matter was taken to independent arbitrator. It was decided that four of the cases should have increases ranging from 28% and 51% but traders are once again claiming that some of them will be forced out of business if comparable increases are demanded from the other fifty cases.

A more unusual reason given for the decline in business was the competition from French markets, together with the one general to all Oxford businesses, high parking charges have left the city centre and have been replaced by chain stores, souvenir shops, fast food outlets and mobile phone centres. Very soon parking in Oxford may cease to be an issue as few people will want to shop there, preferring to go further afield where facilities are so much better.

Although there is seldom an empty unit in the Market, they may in future be occupied by businesses very different indeed from the traditional small, local ones which have been a feature of the site for decades.

Save the Covered Market poster in Nothing, June 2008.

THE MARKET.

1 } Alden, Wm. H.,
2 } butcher
3 } Alden, Isaac
4 } butcher
5 } Jackson, G., butcher
6 } Solloway, M.,
7 } butcher
8 } Woodford, G., butcher
9 } Wixon, W., butcher
10 } Green F., butcher
11 }
12 } Weighing-house
13 } Nix, Robert N., provision merchant
14 } Palmer, J., butcher
15 } Solloway, D., butcher
16 } Alden, Robert R.,
17 } butcher
18 }
19 } Hedges, A.,
20 } butcher
21 } Clarke, W.,provision
22 } dealer, bacon curer, and sausage maker
23 } Hedges, E., butcher
24 } Hatt, J., butcher
25 } Simmonds, F.,
26 } butcher
27 } Hedges, James, bacon curer
28 } Wilkins, W., butcher

29 } Moreton, H., pork butcher, bacon curer
30 } Smith, A., butcher
31 }
32 } **Pigott, E. E.,** provision merchant
33 } Falkner, H.,
34 } butcher
35 } Debron, H. J., pork butcher
36 }
37 } Rose, R., butcher
38 } Gee, John, fruiterer and gardener
39 } Hicks, Thomas, poulterer and dealer in game
40 } Hedges, Mrs, poulterer, game-dealer,
to
43 } and green-grocer
44 } King, W.,bacon curer
45 } Gee, J., fruiterer and greengrocer
46 } Crabb, E., fruiterer
47 } Walklett, F. & G., butchers
48 } Woods, E., butcher
49 } Smith, W., dealer in game
50 } Day, D., florist and
51 } greengrocer
52 }
53 } Poole, J., fruit and potato merchant
54 } Quelch, A., potato merchant
55 } Hemmings, W., greengrocer and butter dealer
56 } Hicks, Thos., poulterer and dealer in game
57 } King, W., bacon curer
58 } Cross, W., confectioner and sweet merchant
59 } Tew, John, fruit and potato merchant
60 } Day, D., florist
61 } Lindsey, J.,
62 } butcher
63 }
64 } Meadows, G, D., provision stores

65 } Simmonds, E. & Son, fruit and potato merchants
66 } The Market Café— Moulder, J., proptr.
67 } Cross, W., confectioner
68 }
69 }
70 } Beckett, C., fruiterer
71 }
72 } Bates, Mr., florist
73 }
74 } Lander, W., greengrocer
75 } Market Café— Moulder, J.
76 } Simmonds, E, and potato
77 } Son fruit and potato merchants
78 } Soden, J., seedsman
79 } Cotmore, Mrs.,greengrocer
80 } Barton, C., greengrocer
81 } Rose, J., bacon
82 } curer
83 } Howse, G. A., butcher
84 } Solloway, J., butcher
85 } Smith, T. J.,
86 } butcher
87 } Woodford, J. E.,
88 } butcher
89 }
90 } Hughes, J., pork butcher and bacon curer
91 }
92 } Solloway,Isaac,butcher
93 }
94 }
95 } Oxford Café—
96 }
97 } Clarke, Mr.
98 }
99 } Mott, F., fruiterer
100 } Narroway, E.,greengrocer
101 } Johnson, Thomas, greengrocer
102 } **Lambourn, G.,** basket maker
to
105 }
106 }
107 } Solloway, D., butcher

108 } Rippington, R., butcher
109 } Holton, W., butcher
110 } Anstey, C. B., florist, &c.
111 } Fortescue, B.,
112 } Solloway, W., butcher
113 } Nix, J., provision merchant
114 } Smart, H., greengrocer
115 } Poole, J., greengrocer
116 } Turrell, T., poulterer and dealer in
117 }
118 } game
119 } Hughes, E., greengrocer &c.
120 } Watts, H., butcher
121 } Hughes, J., greengrocer &c.
122 } Nix, J., provision merchant
123 } Alden, W. H., butcher
124 } Field, Mrs, greengrocer & fruiterer
125 } North, F. & West,
126 } W. G., florists
127 } Eaton, Mr., butcher
128 } Mobley, G., butcher
129 } Griffin, William C., butcher
130 }
131 } Nash, J.,
132 } Barrett, G., greengrocer
133 } Reeve, S., greengrocer
134 } Wakefield, V., greengrocer
135 }
136 } White, J., fruiterer
137 }
138 } Turrill, Joseph, gardener
140 }
142 }
143 }
144 } Sturges, G.,
145 } Harper, W., gardener
146 }
147 }
148 } Webb, J., fruiterer
154 }

155 } Hedges, Mrs.,
to
159 } fruiterer & greengrocer
160 } Smith, A.,green-grocer
161 }
162 } grocer
163 } Reeve, gardener
164 } Salter, G., greengrocer
165 } Beckett, C., greengrocer
166 } grocer & fruiterer
167 }
168 } Bates, Joseph florist
169 }
170 } Walton, Mrs, florist
171 } Robinson, T., greengrocer
to
177 } and fruiterer
178 } Fuller, Jas, greengrocer
179 } Smart, H., greengrocer
180 } Rose, Thos, greengrocer
181 } grocer

Fish Market,

Gray, T. M., fishmonger
Parker, W., fishmonger
Thomas, W. J., fishmonger, fruiterer, & potato merchant
Parker, P. and Son, fishmongers

Market entry in Valter's Post Office Directory 1892

SECTION TWO

Butchers

From the opening of the New Market, the butchers were dominant. These butchery businesses were traditionally the aristocrats of the Covered Market both as regards numbers and longevity. Alden's moved there in 1793 and Lindsey's was opened in 1800. However this concentration of quality meat proved a strong attraction to thieves. In February 1782 for instance, much meat was stolen over the weekend from a stall in the Market and later that year all the meat (to the value of nearly £5), was stolen from one shop. In November 1788 two robbers were sent to Oxford Castle for stealing bacon and cheese from the Market and two years later another butcher's premises were broken into and a lot of meat stolen; 'some of it hidden in a farm-yard near Jericho Gardens, but found by dogs and all gnawed except for one leg of mutton.'

Robson's Directory of Oxford, which classifies traders by occupation instead of location, lists 109 butchery businesses in Oxford in 1858. Of these no fewer than 91 are in the Market and this was before the extensions which were built later in the century. The positions given within the Market are unusual and don't correspond with the normal North, South, East or West Side, straightforward numbering, or Avenues which came later. Instead the Body, Bottom and Middle with ranges as well as sides are marked.

Several names familiar to 20th-century shoppers are among those found in 1858 and include Alden, Hedges and Lindsey, all still in business in Oxford to this day. Of the 18 butchers' shops not situated in the Market itself, all but two have the same surnames as butchers operating inside it and appear to be branches opened in the suburbs.

It is difficult to see how such a large number of traders in the same business managed to make a living (as well as pay relatively high rents) within such a confined space as the Market but they undoubtedly did so as their businesses appear year after year in trade directories and were handed down the generations.

The form of communication known as butchers' back-slang, which is found all over the country, probably predates the Market itself and has persisted to the present day. Like other forms of speech peculiar to a particular group of people, it originated with the intention of allowing speakers to converse openly among themselves in front of those who were not supposed to understand what was being said. It also had the effect of creating a feeling of solidarity among those who spoke it although in the case of the Covered Market butchers these were in such a large majority that this seems hardly necessary. Everyday expressions such as "Flah a gel ebmal" for half a leg of lamb are probably the result of habit but more extreme examples were coined in order to refer to unpopular customers in their hearing and can be very offensive.

Charles Clark butchers' premises photographed in 1909 and inset, advert for William Clark, Butchers, c 1900.

Deliveries to the Meat Market via the High Street in the 1940s; today everything is delivered through Market Street.

WILLIAM H. ALDEN, University & Family Butcher.

Established 1798.

First Quality Meat.

Superior Pickled Beef and Ox Tongues.

Pork and Beef Sausages of the Choicest Quality.

Families regularly waited on for Orders.

67, 68 and 109, The Market, OXFORD.

Advert for Alden's, one of the oldest and best known of Oxford butchery businesses, established in 1793. Alden's claimed to have invented the famous Oxford Sausage

Alden's exterior shown in November 1959. Alden's is still in business as 'catering butchers' but on Osney Mead trading estate.

Two butchers pose behind their window display at Alden's, November 1959.

Mr W M Burrell of R R Alden pictured with a handful of tripe in October 1974.

Richard Alden poses with 17 of the 25 types of sausages on sale in his shop in 1990 when the Great British Banger was said to be under threat from EEC regulations.

1950 Advert for Alec Butterfield butchers' businesses in the Market and in the suburbs.

Butterfield's premises in 1959.

A butcher working in a market meat-store in November 1960.

This couple have plenty to choose from in this window full of everyday meat.

The exterior of Gordon Harris's shop in December 1962.

Good old-fashioned English joints and bangers on display in 1964 before the start of all the regulations which were later to threaten the British meat industry.

This pair of Canadian moose antlers measuring five feet across was mounted outside Richards in July 1965, but not as an advert for moose steaks.

A selection of game and poultry displayed at Richards in December 1982. Since then venison has become a popular meat all the year round, not just in the winter.

Neville Tiller of Richards, when interviewed in March 1989, was just one of the many tenants who complained that rent rises that year were too high.

As Mr Tiller feared, HF Richards shop, shown here in October 1992, was another well-known butcher's which is no longer in business.

More sausages in July 1999, this time at Scoffs, a specialist shop. Here David Walker displays just two of the varieties from the wide range listed on the blackboard behind him.

November 1991. One of the few clues that this business belongs to a butcher is the model to the left of the window. The other goods such as preserves, cheeses, tins of shortbread, and olive oil, make the premises look like a cross between a gift shop and a delicatessen, very different from the traditional carcasses and sawdust. In direct contrast to their predecessors who specialized as pork butchers, bacon curers, tripe dressers, poulterers and game dealers, the four butchers in the Market today offer all kinds of meats, fresh, cured and cooked as well as a range of eggs.

Mark Stoker of Hedges poses with a delivery bike loaded up with meat in September 1994 for an article about rumours that some of the Oxford colleges were planning to take their trade elsewhere. At least one college Bursar feared that certain butchers might be taking advantage of college trade by overcharging.

Barbecue advert at Hedges.

Poster outside Hedges advertising various types of British meat.

Basket of duck eggs in Fellers who have been very successful since they started in the market in 1979 and have won the Organic Retailer of the Year award for meat.

A BRIEF HISTORY OF THE OLDEST HAM IN THE WORLD

This ancient ham came to England in 1892 from Cudahay & Co. of Chicago and was retained as a curiosity by its importer Mr. Arthur M. Barrett, a wholesale provision merchant of Call Lane, Leeds. and hung in his office until 1958 when the business closed down.

The secret of the ham's longevity is due to the borax in which it was cured and is possibly still edible although not guaranteed. The charm remains, for to-day no fly rests on the world's oldest ham.

In 1940 Cudahay & Co. claimed it had the oldest ham in the world. It was insured for $5000. was kept under lock and key and could be seen by appointment only. When the company heard from Mr Barrett that his ham was fifteen years older, it invited the ham to tour America "under a guarantee covering calamity insurance, all expenses paid and safe return", but Mr. Barrett declined.

Since 1958 until Michael Feller bought the ham at Christie's Auction House in 1993 it had been tenderly cared for by Miss D. M. Barrett the daughter of the man who imported it 101 years ago.

The history of the oldest ham in the world displayed at Fellers.

Notice about goat meat at Lindsey and Son. Despite, or perhaps become of, their long associations with the Market, today's butchers keep up with current demands as this sign shows.

David John in Avenue 3 has taken advantage of the fast food and lunch-time trade to offer hot or cold pies and pasties, including an assortment of fruit pies.

Fruit, Vegetables and Flowers

From the early days of the Market, the florists, seeds-men, fruiterers and greengrocers have been found dotted between the various types of butcher.

Florists' names which were to be found until recently include Field, Jacob and West (who had a garden centre in Windmill Road, Headington, until 2005). Today there are two florists in the market, Jemini and the Garden.

Fruiterers and greengrocers were Yeates, Goodeys, Mortimers, Smarts, Tyrells, Hedges and Durhams. The present-day businesses are McCarthy's and Bonner's.

The seedmen had market gardens and nurseries in the suburbs, notably in Summertown, and gardeners, both professional and amateur, could buy seeds and plants ready to take out. Gardening enjoyed a huge increase in popularity in the course of the 19th century and some of the suppliers such as the Bates, Days, Dunbars, Gees and Kilbees were well known locally.

Gee's glasshouse turned restaurant. The long-standing Gee family business, which was eventually taken over by Butterfield's and included a fruiterer's, is commemorated in Gee's restaurant in the Banbury Road which is housed in a very ornate Victorian former glasshouse.

PHONE: *Private Ex.* 2283 *and* 2809

CHARLES GEE & SONS

(ALEC. R. BUTTERFIELD)

Fruiterers, Greengrocers and Italian Warehousemen

THE MARKET, OXFORD

Grocery Branch: HOOPERS, Rose Hill   *Phone* 77564

We always have the best selection of Fruit and Vegetables from Covent Garden and Local Growers

1950 Advert for Charles Gee and Sons, by then run by butcher Alec Butterfield.

Mr Ted Titcomb shown in December 1955 in the cellars under the Covered Market, attending to the bananas being ripened there. In the war years bananas became something of a rarity but there were plenty to go round, in Oxford at least, by the mid-Fifties. As many as 600 bunches could be stored at a time in the cellar where the temperature could be kept at a moist, even 68-70% to ripen them. Gas heating was found to the best and the air was sprayed from time to time to keep the right humidity. In the mid-Fifties, bananas were one of the best buys as regards fresh fruit and cost 1/4d (about 6p) a pound but were said to be of inferior taste to those around before the War. They came from Jamaica and had almost replaced the smaller and spottier Canary variety whose appearance just didn't appeal to buyers.

Apples were imported from the USA, Canada and Europe, grapes from Spain and Holland and dates and nuts from various hotter countries. Greengrocers remarked that the British public was more interested in price and appearance that taste and quality, having perhaps 'lost its palate' during the War when people had to eat what was available.

One trader even said 'About the only people who understand fruit now are the aristocracy in their 80s. The educated palate has almost disappeared'.

Henry Smart and Sons Ltd in December 1958. Fred Smart, who had been working in the family firm since about 1910, spoke about long working hours when the Market didn't close on Saturdays until midnight and even in the late Thirties it stayed open until 9 pm. He recalled how, before the Great War, the Market had a 'floating population of hangers-on' who used to try to earn a few pennies by holding horses or carrying heavy loads, and then sleep rough. He also remembers how the Clerks of the Market would do their rounds weighing butter and other commodities.

Among some of the interesting fruit prices in August 1960 are peaches and grapefruit at 9d [4½p] each.

A well-stocked fruit stall in December 1960. Note the unusual location of the City of Oxford Electricity Supply Department's showrooms in the background.

It seems that there was a shortage of sprouts in January 1963, no doubt caused by the unusually harsh winter that year.

Something of an innovation at the time, ready-prepared vegetables being advertised in December 1964.

Like any other Oxford business, the Market's shops and stalls are under the City Council's jurisdiction as regards opening hours. The Deputy Chief Inspector of Weights and Measures, JHB Hornby is shown discussing a poll concerning the abolition of the early closing day with fruiterer Mr FG Mortimer in May 1965.

Self-selection was a new concept in buying fruit in September 1980; it did away with complaints about serving inferior produce from the back of the stall but customers needed to have long arms to reach everything they wanted.

The opening ceremony of the refurbished Durham's fruiterers in June 1988 was performed by Bully, a four-year-old African elephant. Bully's payment was in apples, cabbages and other produce from the stall. Pictured with Bully are his handler, Glyn Picton and Peter Durham. The elephant's appearance provoked complaints from animal lovers who pointed out that circuses including performing animals had been banned by the council and that the Covered Market was council property.

In July 1983 fruiterer Mick McCarthy noted a welcome increase in trade thanks to the hot weather when he sold lots of peaches, melons and strawberries.

Bonner's shown in June 1991 looks very similar to how it does today.

A fine display of chrysanthemums and houseplants in 1956.

Another of the florist's shops for which the Market has always been noted, shown in December 1957.

MEMBERS OF

INTERFLORA
WE TELEGRAPH FLOWERS

INTERFLORA

S. WEST & SONS

Florists

Seedsmen   :   Nurserymen

THE MARKET - OXFORD

PHONE 48637

20 BROAD STREET   74 WINDMILL ROAD

Advert for West's, 1958. The Windmill Road nurseries and garden centre continued in business until July 2005.

In December 1959 florists were very evident in this Avenue; West's was one of the best known and longest lasting, listed in directories as 'West, W.G. & S., nurserymen and florists, Old Headington, and at 125 and 126 The Market, Oxford'.

According to the Oxford Mail reporter, this shop belonging to old-established firm Field and Jacob was one of the most attractive in the Market in December 1960.

Another view of Field and Jacob, taken in December 1964

The Waterperry Horticultural Centre shop, which had been in the Market for about thirty years, closed to the public in July 1983. Along with other traders, the shop had been badly hit by parking restrictions and rising rents.

A 1976 Advert for Jemini.

Jemini flower girls celebrating the 200th anniversary of the Market in November 1990 are, left to right, Michelle Clements, Janette Edwards, Rachel Jaques, Chris Simpson, Caroline Ayres (at back) and Tania Trinder. Jemini have won the Gold Medal at Chelsea on three occasions, each time also winning the prized Chelsea Cup

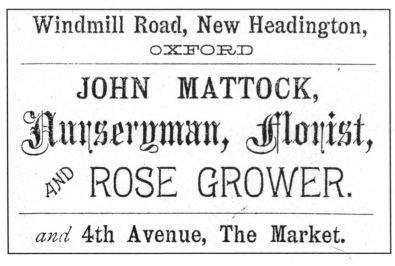

Windmill Road, New Headington, OXFORD

JOHN MATTOCK,

Nurseryman, Florist,

AND ROSE GROWER.

and 4th Avenue, The Market.

The Mattock family continued to grow roses at Headington until the late 20th century when Mattock Close was built on the site of their nursery. However, Robert Mattock still grows roses at Abingdon.

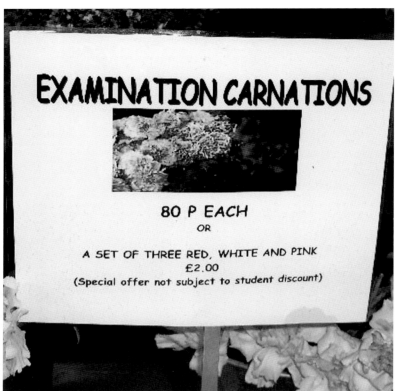

Carnation button-holes on sale at Jemini. At examination time hundreds of students buy button-holes (normally carnations) which are worn with full academic dress when taking Final exams. The flowers are colour-coded starting with white ones for the first paper and ending with deep red for the last.

The Garden, successor to the Waterperry shop, shown in September 1994..

Fish and other Foodstuffs

Along with the butchers, fishmongers have also been in the Market from its early days when they moved from Fish Street (St Aldates). Despite being founder-tenants, the fish-mongers at the north end of the Market were out in the open until the construction of the present wall and roof extension bordering Market Street in 1900 and have never been very numerous. Among well known fishmongers were Parkers and Byards.

This picture of 3-year-old David Allen attempting to land a giant halibut was taken in August 1970.

A return to the bad old days of theft from the Market took place in the mid-1970s when two fishmongers, Cypera and Hayman's, lost about £1000 worth of stock in a year. Thieves were able to get away with the fish because it was left outside the locked gates by the distributors late at night before the stall-holders arrived for work in the morning. In March 1975 about 12 stone of smoked fish was taken. The increase in home freezers had made the frozen fish much more attractive.

Douglas Stevens, manager of Cypera, with a half-empty slab

Bill Hayman showing the empty slab on his stall in March 1975 after fish thieves had struck.

Fishy faces (and low prices) in the Market in October 1978.

A novelty at Hayman's in July 1995 was this shark posing with Lionel Evans who said he was often asked to let tourists take his photo with the fish.

In November 1987 alligator meat was being promoted by Andrew Russell of Hayman's.

Today Hayman's Fisheries, run by Richard Alden, chairman of the Covered Market Traders' Association, is the only surviving fishmonger in the Market. It is the city's leading independent supplier of fresh fish, offering up to 80 different types. Their website entry claims that 'our skilled fishmongers can speak 5 different languages'.

Christmas carp at Hayman's 2007. Carp has become more popular than fresh salmon in Oxford. This is due to the increasing number of Eastern Europeans settling in the city, in particular Poles. Manager Ray Lindsey says that Hayman's have been supplying carp for the last 12 years and expected to sell 500 kilos of carp at Christmas, with a turnover of nearly £4,500. Poles eat carp over the festive season as part of a meal called Wigilia on Christmas Eve, because the sign of the fish represents Christ. Most of Hayman's carp comes from Holland where it is farmed so it doesn't taste as earthy as British fish which come from rivers and lakes.

From the opening of the Market, the Clerks of the Market went into action to ensure fair trading and that the laws relating to trading there were strictly observed. *Jackson's Oxford Journal* kept citizens abreast with their activities.

In 1782 for example, it carries an announcement made by William Elias Taunton, Clerk of the Market and also a Clerk of the Peace, to the effect that anyone offering butter for sale outside the market was to be prosecuted for doing so. There are numerous examples of the price of bread being fixed by the Clerks. That the Clerks' edicts were to be taken seriously is shown by the notice on 8th March 1783 that the Clerks had recently seized a quantity of butter 'deficient in weight' which was to be distributed among the poor.

Never numerous, perhaps because of the attentions of the Clerks of the Market, former bakers included Pusey, Drewitt and Parslow's of Reading. The exterior of the Market's surviving general baker, Nash's.

A modern variant on an old theme, Ben's Cookies in the 1990s. The Oxford shop, opened in 1984, was the original, since then there are more outlets in the UK as well as in the USA and on-line.

The Oxford Cheese Company's shop in the 1990s. It is still going strong and has been able to concentrate solely on cheese sales. Cheesemongers (or factors) are rare, one example being George Brown in the 1840s. Cheese was also sold by butchers, dairymen, general provision merchants, and, more recently, delicatessens. The Cheese Company's website describes its pride and joy: *Oxford Blue is made entirely by hand to our specifications in a leading Stilton dairy.* The World Encyclopedia of Cheese describes Oxford Blue - *'When ripe, the cheese is a luscious creamy blue with distinct but not strong blue flavour. Aromatic and spicy, it has a hint of dark chocolate and white wine, with tarragon on the finish.*

Knight's shop window displaying a variety of cheeses, tinned food and sauces on sale in 1957.

December 1960 and an early example of a delicatessen, its contents on sale along with more everyday goods such as Corn Flakes and porridge.

Palm's delivery bike

*They're
usually
busy
at
Palm's
. . . .*

*. . . . but
never
too busy
to give
pleasant
service!*

For the rarest of delicacies and most luxurious foods, fruits and vegetables—

PALM'S DELICATESSEN

84 Covered Market   Oxford 47500

SUCH RARITIES AS
FROZEN FROG LEGS
AND PREPARED
ESCARGOTS;
AMERICAN
BAKING CHOC.,
ETC.

SLIMMING NOURISHING
FOODS A SPECIALITY

CONTINENTAL
AND
AMERICAN FOODS,
INDIAN SPICES,
CHINESE DAINTIES
AND CHOICEST
CHEESE

ORDERS DELIVERED
LOCALLY
BY ARRANGEMENT

ALL LOCAL BUSES
STOP NEAR
THE MARKET

Advert for Palm's Delicatessen, 1967. Palm's sums up the atmosphere of the modern Market where it has become something of an icon.

Inside Palm's in May 1981.

In December 1966 the Women's Institute's Market shop received nearly 50 orders for Christmas cakes, 80 for turkeys and chickens and about 200 for mince pies. The shop, which was staffed by volunteers, moved from a stall in the Oxpens market into the Covered Market in 1946. The produce, which was home-made, came from WI members all over Oxfordshire and North Berkshire. Members received all the cash taken apart from a penny in the shilling which went towards paying the rent on the shop.

Fasta Pasta opened in October 1983, complete with a machine which could turn out all pasta shapes. Shown trying it out are, from the left, Penny Everard, Francis Rockliff and Sally von Meister.

December 1959 the Sweet Shop. Confectioners listed in trade directories over the years included Cross's, Curtis's, Finch's, Gibbs's, Seaton's, Nicholson's, Annett's and Ward's which is still in business today as a newsagents and sandwich bar as well as a sweetshop.

Cafés, restaurants and eating-houses have been a feature of the Market since the later part of the nineteenth century. In the 1880s the Market Café was kept by the unfortunately named Mr Moulder, in premises at numbers 75 and 95-6. The customers at early eateries were probably fellow traders. In the early 1900s the Market Refreshment Rooms managed by James Hunt, and Mrs George's dining rooms sound much more genteel. Moving on to the Twenties one finds that Miss Brown has also opened dining rooms at numbers 92 and 128-130. In the Sixties, Hunt's Café is at numbers 5-8, Brown's still in the same place and George's Café at 15-16. In the mid-70s George's is listed as 77a-80. It was not until the sudden expansion of fast-food market in the late-20th century, however, that the Covered Market became a major focus of eateries, with cafés, sandwich bars, coffee shops, cookie and milkshake providers, patisseries, health eating outlets as well as Brown's which is still serving old-fashioned sit-down meals.

The exterior of Brown's Café in April 1993; little has changed today.

Queuing for sandwiches at Hunt's in September 1980. At one time queuing or even attendance in person wasn't necessary as Hunt's offered a delivery service to office workers who ordered in advance from the café's lunch-time menu.

Interior of George's in July 1976. George's was named for the family, a member of which Mrs Amos George, ran it for 56 years. In 1954, the café was taken over by John Bird, a former market butcher, and by 1968 it was serving more than 100 lunches a day. Jan Morris describes it in her book *Oxford*, as it was in the mid-1960s. Customers included survivors from college balls, Mrs Mops, labourers, Asian bus-conductors German hitch-hikers as well as the market traders themselves. George's was known for its use of mugs rather than cups, its dripping toast and the size of its breakfasts. The café continues today under the name Georgina's and is much more upmarket.

Beaton's takeaway in November 1993.

The counter at Georgina's in October 1989.

Exterior of Cardew's. The aroma of roasting coffee would be near the top of most people's list of the attractions of the Covered Market. In 1965 Cardew and Co. moved into the Market from St Michaels Street where it had opened in 1948. Many of Cardew's oldest customers, who live all over the world, have been shopping there since their student days. With only two shops (the other is in Cambridge), Cardew's is able to build up a personal rapport with its customers.

Sofi de France is typical of today's eateries where customers can get freshly-prepared snacks or sit down for a more leisurely break.

Chocology, which John Partington founded in 2000, is one of the Covered Market's success stories. The first shop was opened in 2001 to offer high quality continental chocolates and soon attracted several Oxford colleges and companies as customers. The following year a second shop opened at London Bridge Station followed by another at Euston Station in 2003. The Oxford shop has been extended to include a bar serving hot chocolate. It has held an Easter Egg Extravaganza and Halloween Hat Hunt as well as combining with a cinema to advertise the film *Chocolat*. Chocology has featured on the television programme *Nosh* and appeared in *What's on in London* and the BBC *Good Homes Magazine*.

Another achiever is the Cake Shop where enthusiasts are usually to be found gazing admiringly through the windows. At one end the cake decorators are busy creating their masterpieces from start to finish and at the other are displays of the completed products. These spectacular cakes are more than works of art because they are so imaginative, ranging from personalized birthday cakes, to gifts from Oxford, and really original examples of wedding cakes such as an entire top table, an Afro-Caribbean bride and groom and even two male partners in a civil ceremony. The Cake Shop's windows certainly are visitor attractions in their own right.

Wedding Cakes

Clothing, Footwear and Accessories

The ladies' wear on this stall is typical of those found in any market stall in the country at that time, December 1955, and very different from the trendy fashions that were to appear later in the Market's boutiques.

Elegant dresses at Thena boutique which, says its website, 'links with the dynamic world of ladies fashion in South East Asia' and offers stylish clothing including evening, party and casual wear.

Ladies' clothing on sale in December 1958.

Two women students choosing nylon stockings in the pre-tights era. Prices ranged from about 15p to 40p a pair in December 1962.

In the 1920s Arthur Pedder had a millinery business in the Market. This rather drab collection dates from 1967 but today the Hat Box in Avenue 3 caters for both men and women including, says its website 'cocktail fascinators by the best of British designers' as well as a tailor-made service.

January 1978 and publicity for a competition arranged by Watson's, who were offering free pairs of jeans as prizes, included this 10' high robot made of fibre glass and steel but manned by a human inside it. Admiring the figure are Patsy Curtin, Susan Davis and Wendy Hazell. In the 1940s Arnold Watson had run a hosiery business in the Market.

Nothing and Next to Nothing in June 1992.

Knitwear and Jewellery in November 1992.

Lucy Clacher (left) and Emily Chandler surrounded by some of the treasures on sale at Bangles in June 1999.

Campus Stores offered a whole range of University-related items and souvenirs ranging from sweat-shirts, tee-shirts, and mugs to teddy bears.

A boot sign reminiscent of those hung outside businesses to alert the illiterate to the trade carried on in the premises below. Earlier boot and shoes businesses were Gould and Thomas, both shoemakers in the 1840s, Austin, bootmaker in the Sixties and Jimmy Mac Shoes in the Seventies. Jimmy Mac was the forerunner to Macsamillion Ltd; although Jimmy Mac Shoes was located on Avenue 4, where Two Foot Nothing is now. When the Jimmy Mac shop, was sold, the business moved to 11-15 Avenue 1 and became Macsamillion of Oxford.

April 1993, Macsamillion which claims to offer 'the ultimate in men's classic footwear' with a host of leading brands and a wide selection of Italian shoes. The Oxford Boot Store, which has the same owners, is also in Avenue 1, near the High Street entrance.

The Oxford Cobbler in December 1988 with Stacey Weeks (centre) with Paul Mason , John Dyer and Tony Ashworth.

This selection of bags and cases at Delcoy's was photographed in the early Sixties.

November 1984, gloves and bags in Delcoy's. The shop was described as 'Oxford's treasure chest of luggage' when it opened a glove and handbag boutique which offered hand-measuring and 24-hour delivery services. Prices ranged from £1.25 for nylon gloves to £60 for top quality leather ones. Alfred Delcoy said that there was a demand for fingerless gloves from his fellow-traders. In the 1960s Delcoy had two outfitter's premises.

Both Fellers and Bonners now offer environmentally friendly and reusable bags.

84 MAR   OXFORD STREET DIRECTORY.

MANSFIELD ROAD—con.
......*here is Jowett walk*......
University of Oxford
  Clerk of Works (yard)
1 Etheridge Frank, university lodging house

THE MARKET (Market street).

1 Fortescue Miss L. M. florist
2 Gibbs Frederick William, wholesale confectionr
3 & 4 Lindsey W.L. butchr
5 & 6 Hunt James, refreshment rooms
7 & 8 Lambourn & Co. basket makers
9, 10, 11 & 12 Mortimer F. J. fruiterer
13 & 14 Clarke Miss S. C. greengrocer
15 & 16 George Mrs. A. J. dining rooms
16 Brown Frank R. dog requisites dealer
17, 18 & 19 Gower E. fishmonger
20 & 49 Cooper J. & Son, fruitrs
  Cutting Walt. H. confr
21, 22 & 23 Pigott & Son, wholesale provision merchants & bacon curers. Tel. 516
24, 25, 26 & 27 **MARTIN & GODDARD,** pork butchers
28, 29, 40 & 41 Turrill James & Walter, poulterers
30 & 31 Poole John, grngro
32, 33 & 34, 52, 62 & 90 & 91 **SMART HENRY & SONS,** fruiterers
35, 36, 37 & 39 West & Sons, florists
38, 58 & 65 & 66 Alden Ernest & Son, btchrs
39 West & Sons, florists
40, 41, 28 & 29 Turrill James & Walter, poulterers
42 & 43 Turrill J. & Son, btchrs
44 & 45 Steventon William, butcher
46, 47, 48 & 53 **LINDSEY JOHN & SON,** btchrs
49 & 20 Cooper J. & Son, fruitrs

50 & 51 Parker Peter & Son, fishmongers
52 & 32, 33, 34, 62, 90 & 91 Smart Henry & Sons, fruiterers
53, 46, 47 & 48 Lindsey John & Son, butchers
54 to 56 Brewer William & Sons, fruiterers
57 & 84, 85, 86 & 94 Gee Charles & Sons, grngros
58 Alden Ernest & Son, butchers
60 Butterfield Mrs. R. A. butcher
62, 32, 33 & 34 Smart Hy. & Sons, fruiterers
64 Bowley V. & W. fruitrs
65, 66 & 38 & 58 Alden Ernest & Son, butchrs
67 & 68, 72 to 77 & 108 & 109 **ALDEN ROBERT R. & SON,** btchrs. See advt
69, 70 & 71. **FIELD & JACOB,** the noted shop for floral designs. Tel. 291
72 to 77 & 67, 68 & 108 & 109 **ALDEN ROBERT R. & SON,** pork butchers & butchers. Telephone No. 33. See advertisement
78, 79 & 80 Alden Cyril & Sons, butchers
81 & 82 Gibbard Edward, butcher
84, 85, 86, 57 & 94 Gee Chas. & Sons, grngros
87 & 88 & 93 Tyrrell Hy. fruiterer
89 Chambers Tobias Alban, market gardener
94, 84, 85, 86 & 57 Gee Chas. & Sons, grngros
90 & 91 & 32, 33, 34, 52 & 62 Smart Henry & Sons, fruiterers
93, 87 & 88 Tyrrell Henry, fruiterer
92 Brown Miss S. C. L. dining rooms
95, 96 & 97 **RICHARDS H. F.** poulterer, game dealer & provision merchant. Telephone 89

99 & 100 Clark Charles W. pork butcher
101, 102, 103 & 103A, **KNIGHT EDWARD,** cheese & bacon factor. Telephone 217
104 & 105 Hedges E. & Sons, butchers
107 Levett Fredk. C. florist
108 & 109, 67 & 68 & 72 to 77 Alden Robert R. & Son, btchrs. See advt
110, 111 & 112 Goodey S. & Sons, fruiterers
112A, Seatons Ltd. confrs
113, 114, 115 & 116 Goodey S. & Sons, florists
116A, Felton Bros. drapers
117 Butterfield Mrs. R. A. butcher
  Dead Weight Office
118 & 148 & 149 Walker Charles, toy dealer
119 Hall Mrs. F. greengrcr
120 Pedder Arthur, millnr
121 Hedges Mrs. C. poulterer
123 & 124 & 143, 144 & 145 Hedges Mrs. M. fruiterer
125 Darcey A. & Son, oil & color merchants
126 Goodey W. & Sons, fruitrs
127 Tyrell Henry, fruiterer
128, 129 & 130 Brown Miss S. C. L. dining rooms
130 Allee Chas. W. N. btchr
131, 132, 133 & 134 Oxfordshire Farmers Bacon Factory Ltd. bacon by-products
135 to 138 Durham's, fruitrs
139 Goodey W. & Sons, fruitrs
140, 141 & 142 Darcey A. & Son, who. toy mers
143, 144 & 145 & 123 & 124 Hedges Mrs. M. fruitr
148 & 149 & 118 Walker Charles, toy dealer
152 Druce M. J. greengrocr
153 Heritage Mrs. poulterer
155 Turrill Harry, fruiterer
156 Reeley Miss, bookseller

Market buildings.
See MARKET STREET.

Market entry in Kelly's Directory for 1926.

Household and Lifestyle

Over the years the number of stalls and shops which sold goods other than foodstuffs gradually increased. The earliest of these, like the warehouse stocking sacks, woollen cloth and tarpaulins advertised in Jackson's Oxford Journal in 1782, were practical items. Also available were baskets to carry away one's purchases, earthenware cooking dishes and glassware.

Rolls of household furnishings, including carpets, on sale in December 1964.

Towels and household linen in December 1957 at a conventional market stall.

More rolls of material in December 1962. In the 1920s Felton Brothers had a drapers business in the Market, as did Bowen's in the 1970s. In 1940s this shop was trading as Lazarus Luck, textiles, and there was also Durrant's in the 1960s.

Materials piled up to the ceiling at Luck's in December 1964.

Baskets galore outside Brown's in December 1964. The company was set up in 1890 and still trades as CH Brown and Son. The present very successful business has been developed by Mike and Sue Norton and their daughters, all the family being experienced in designing, making and repairing saddles, indeed their website is saddledoctors.uk. Apart from offering a selection of more than 200 saddles Brown's stocks top of the range leather goods: handbags, wallets, luggage, riding and country wear, baskets and posh wellies.

Brown's saddlers interior July 1976. As early as 1783 a saddler and cap-maker opened a shop in the Market.

Another picture of Delcoy's, taken in November 1992 when they had been trading in the Market for about thirty four years having moved to that site in the mid-Seventies. They were best known for their selection of trunks.

In December 2001 the opening of the Market Barber in the premises which had previously been Delcoy's, was marked by a performance by Wheatley barber shop quartet Short Back and Sides. From left: Mike Hogan, Dan Wilkinson, David Willcock and Malcolm Benson.

The staff of Lesandon, one of four shops of that name, on their move to larger premises within the Market in November 1970.

A. DARCEY & SON,

125 The Market,

for the latest

TOYS and NOVELTIES.

Come and see our wonderful range of

DOLLS

Dressed and undressed.

Wholesale and Retail.

A mid-1930s advert for Darcey's wholesale toys and novelties. In the 1920s Darcey's was listed in trade directories as an oil and colour merchants and by the 1940s they were trading as glass merchants from a second premises. Other toy shops were owned by Charles Walker, toy dealer owning premises in the 1920s and Foster's toys in the 1960s.

Toys and Models in Collector's Corner, an up-to-date toy and model shop.

Elvis was obviously the King of this record stall in December 1962 if the selection of his LPs is anything to go by. The number one single that Christmas was Elvis's *Return to Sender*.

In 1962, before the Sixties had got into full swing, both the recording and the buying of gramophone records was an almost exclusively adult business. There were three types of record, all of them relatively expensive to buy and, being made of plastic, very easy to scratch or break. The largest were the 33 rpm LPs (albums) and the most common the 45 rpm singles. Between them were the EPs (extended play) which had 4 tracks, but these never became really popular.

The lady in record stall in the photograph is surrounded by the best-selling LPs of that Christmas, almost all of which were by mature singers, Elvis and Bobby Vee being the exception. Among them can be seen Pearl Carr and Teddy Johnson, Nina and Frederick, piano-wizard Russ Conway, and the George Mitchell ('Black and White') Minstrels who were extremely popular at the time and had their own television show on which the Two Ronnies got their first big break.

There were two other record sellers in Oxford, Russell Acott in the High Street and Taphouse's in Magdalen Street, both of which dealt in musical instruments, music scores and classical recordings. This little market stall was much less intimidating as it only stocked pop records and potential customers could see at a glance what was available.

Levett's Pet Shop July 1976. In the1940s Frederick Levett, a florist, opened his pet stores. His daughter, Miss Florence Levett, ran Field and Jacob Florists, which had family connections stretching back 150 years, as well as Levett's Pet Shop for nearly 50 years until her death at the age of 98. Miss Levett came back from Australia to take over the family business when her father died in 1947 and began to go up to Covent Garden first thing in the morning in order to select the finest flowers for the shop. Another of her accomplishments was the provision of flowers for May balls and the arrangement of window boxes for some of the colleges. Not surprisingly it was rumoured that Miss Levett didn't take a holiday for over forty years. The shop is now Price's Pets. A similar business in the 1920s was Brown's, listed in directories as a 'dog requisites dealer'.

November 1992 knick-knacks and novelties. The items for sale are very different from those on sale in the mid-1840s at Ashley's china and glass shop, Peake and Owen's hardware and Gibbon's earthenware.

Unusual salt and pepper sets in Red Opia.

Market News, another long-established business. In the 1920s a Miss Reeley sold books in the Market, and in the Forties Ernest Barguss, ran a library there; Mr Barguss's business, however, had become a tobacconist by the Sixties.

Browsers looking at books and records in 1980. This picture accompanied an article in the *Oxford Times* of 19th September entitled *The quaint old world of the Covered Market*. The writer noted that, *Today the Fourth Avenue is largely clothes shops but all the avenues are higgledy-piggledy and mixed.* In 1980 the Market included a jeweller, pet shop, stationer, 3 cafes, 7 butchers, poultry and game dealers, saddlers, tea and coffee merchant, two fishmongers, book-shop, boot shop, 2 florists, and 5 greengrocers. The writer concluded *In 20 years it will be gone or just boutiques for foreigners but if you call yourself an Oxonian you should know it.*

These comments from the *Oxford Times* give food for thought. The words 'quaint old-world' seem light years away from the Market as it is today when its atmosphere is traditional over-laid with brightness and modernity.

The shops in the Covered Market today are not all that different from those to be found there in 1980 and those 'boutiques for foreigners' that he sees as an alternative to closure have not materialized. True Oxonians certainly do know about all that the Covered Market has to offer as the daily queues for lunch-time food and the full Saturday-morning shopping bags prove. How it has all changed since 1852 when the entry in Gardner's Directory read:

Market&–The General Market which extends from the High-street to Market-street, was built from a plan by Mr. Gwynne, architect of Magdalen-bridge, and opened. in 1774, in conformity with an act of parliament obtained in. 1771, for paving and lighting the streets, and for erecting a new market. This act was renewed with some additional clauses in 1836. The market, has several entrances, each secured by an iron gate, and has been much enlarged and improved of late years. It is arranged into three divisions for the departments respectively of butcher's meat, poultry, fruit and vegetables, and is one of the best supplied and best regulated markets in the kingdom. The market-days are *Wednesday* and *Saturday*. Previously to the erection of this market, separate markets for the different articles of consumption were held in various parts of the city, all of which are now, except the corn market, merged into this general one. The present market occupies the site of several academic halls, and the *Apothecaria* and *Spiceria* or market for drugs and spices.

Still going strong, in October 2001, Tony Shepherd and Matt Payne pose outside the Oxford Engraver which had moved from just inside the High Street entrance into one double and one single unit in Avenues 1 and 2.

Charity shops are in every High Street nowadays, but few if any in covered markets elsewhere. Helen and Douglas Houses are hospices in East Oxford caring for terminally ill children and young adults.

Christmas in the Market

The Covered Market always comes into its own over the Christmas period and it is no coincidence that many surviving photographs were taken at that time of year. Although it is clear that today all the employees go to great lengths to make it an attractive, welcoming place, in the early years of the last century Christmas was a time of hard work and long days, sometimes as much as 90 hours. In a series of interviews in the *Oxford Times* in December 1961, traders remembered the good old days.

Vic White, who had worked at his butcher's shop since 1916, recalled *The week before Christmas we used to start at 6 a.m. and finish after 10 p.m. Things will be a bit different this year though, 60 hours a week with be the limit.*

The owner of H Durham and Son, fruiterers, was 13 when he started in the Market. *We worked until 10 p.m. just before Christmas. Oranges used to sell at ten to twenty for a shilling and Cox's Orange Pippins were about 8d a pound.* He went on to say that mixed nuts, oranges and muscatels were among the current Christmas favourites.

Another butcher, Alec Butterfield, agreed about the long hours. *Nowadays we finish at five in the afternoon but there as a time when our busiest time was from 5 o'clock onwards. I remember once in the war years I had to deliver a turkey to a customer at two in the morning!* In 1961 oven-ready turkeys, chickens and pheasants costing form 25/- to 30/- a brace were available.

The *Oxford Mail*, of Saturday 24th December 1938, reported approvingly:
It is good news that the Basque children, who are still living in this district [in Thame and at Aston, Bampton] *will be well provided for this Christmas. Again the Oxford Covered Market Tradesmen, led by Messrs. Charles Evans and Smart, have shown their great generosity by giving large quantities of meat and vegetables, whilst Messrs. Ryard, who have provided fish twice a week since the children arrived at Aston, have now added a turkey to their invaluable gifts.*
Meanwhile many private individuals have rallied round with games and toys, while many contributions have been earmarked for crackers.
It is good to know of so much kindliness, especially at a time when it is not easy for anybody.

Just after World War II, when poultry was still scarce, even a large dealer would think himself lucky to be able to get hold of more than about 20 turkeys and 200 chickens at Christmas. By 1955 however, Oxfordshire had become one of the leading turkey-breeding areas in the country and this meant a wide choice of birds for the consumer. That year dealers estimated that they would be able to sell some 500 turkeys, 1500 chickens, 150 geese and 50 brace of pheasants. Capons weighing 8 or 9 lbs were reckoned as being almost as good value as a small turkey.

Christmas poultry in December 1963. By then oven-ready turkeys were available (although the fresh ones were more popular) and pheasants cost between 25s and 30s (£1.25 and £1.50) a brace. Fish was also very much in demand for an easy to cook pre-Christmas meal.

Unaware of the camera, this lady inspecting a window full of Christmas meats was photographed in December 1960.

Pig carcases were a prominent feature of this butcher's Christmas display in 1964.

Queues in the Market in December 1964 soon after it was confirmed that it would stay on the site that it had occupied for almost two centuries. The newspaper reporter states that far from meaning that service was slow, the queues show that the quality of the goods on sale was worth waiting for. Despite criticisms on traffic grounds, the Buchanan Report found that it was just the sort of pedestrianized shopping area which cities should encourage.

Christmas fruit and nuts in December 1964.

Fresh supplies of fruit being rushed in along Market Street in 1964.

Women looking at very practical gifts in 1963

Apart from the displays of poultry and game, the Covered Market has become well known for its Christmas decorations which in recent years have outshone those in the rest of central Oxford. When lit by Christmas lights, the high roof and narrow Avenues take on a rather theatrical aspect.

Balloons in place in the roof of the Market, Christmas 1961.

Ray and Molly Milton in the banana store under the Market, blowing up the balloons which formed part of the decorations in 1961.

Other Christmas decorations being put up in the roof of the Market in November 1962.

John Reed, a member of the Market Tenants' Association puts the fairy on top of the Market Christmas tree in November 1962.

THE RT. WORSHIPFUL THE
LORD MAYOR OF OXFORD

The Market's Christmas lights being switched on by the Lord Mayor, Alderman Evan Roberts, in November 1962. The lights were provided by the Market Tenants' Association and cost nearly £400. As in previous years, shoppers were requested to hang presents for orphaned and sick children and for the elderly, on the Christmas tree in the centre. As hoped, these exceeded the record 2,300 presents donated in 1960.

A crowd of chilly shoppers patiently waiting for the lights to be switched on in November 1962.

A selection of the Christmas gifts which had been collected for children and elderly people being eyed by prospective recipients in 1966. Along with the Salvation Army officer is a nun from Nazareth House children's home.

1965: Children from Nazareth House sign a Christmas card for local celebrity Jimmy Dingle who had collapsed after appearing as Father Christmas in the Market and had to be taken to the Radcliffe Infirmary. Wearing the Viking helmet is John Reed who organised the collection of presents for the children and old age pensioners.

George Langford taking the early shift at playing Father Christmas in 1969. He was one of a dozen Santas that year. With Mr Langford are, from the left, John Read, organiser of the annual gift appeal, Frank Watts, Walter Denton, Ernest Bursnoll, Brigadier Frank Ellingham of the Salvation Army and Ray Bondsey, manager of Hedges Brothers who gave the 30-foot tree. The young visitors are Alan Cheeseman aged 3 and Benjamin Ganly aged 2.

Winners of the 1993 Grand Christmas draw receiving their prizes from Frank Watson, Chairman of the Tenants' Association. Natasha Wyatt won a mountain bike and Mr and Mrs Les Newport a holiday voucher.